Biography of

A Girl Who Lived

Paperback ISBN: 979-8-9913670-1-1

A note from the author

I made a deal when I was fourteen to never expose my monsters, and I have been a prostitute to that silence my whole life. Left unsatiated, I've drowned in her waters. And no one noticed, especially since I was old enough to swim alone.

This is not a book for the light of heart, straight forward, logistical, statistical, judgmental, or political mind. This book is madness. Trauma. Realization. Rage. Relief. A bound model of my coping mechanism: writing.

There's a kaleidoscope of discovery and pain within these pages. The views and opinions from a naïve child with a narrow world view, who was growing, breaking, and learning with exposure. I'm still learning, years later.

Several themes may shock or disturb some readers. I urge you to prioritize your well-being and comfort zones, as reading is supposed to be a pleasantry, not cause pain. And for those of you who may find these words resonating somewhere deep, see this as physical proof that you are not alone.

~Nightshade

The Saviors Daughter (14)

I hurt everyone around me because I'm too afraid

But still I fight, yet my hope and spirit frayed

I'm a broken girl, tattered and torn

Persistent still though my spirit is worn

Through all the pain hope seems lost

Yet I still look to you hanging off the cross

And still you ignore my pleading cry

While I myself refuse to die

The Split (age 16)

The weight of my life crushes me like the sky.

On my knees, on one foot, one more step,

I'm fine.

Do I go left or right, whose house do I choose?

My brain doesn't work, my soul's been abused.

Who's been making the decisions for me and my life?

On a screen which is splitting I see a husband and wife,

Gold bands on their fingers going black with age,

erupting a demon cackling with rage.

It's a shadow, a ghoul, an unnamed disease,

which takes life so quickly with no hinting sneeze.

Betrayal

Farse vows

My voice clearly unable to stable,

to penetrate the shield of sickening death by their doors.

My worrisome thoughts of who wants it more.

Distractions and promises coming off my tongue feel distasteful,

how much will I lose, how much more disabled?

Pens break in my hand covering paper in blood,

losing beams of support and faint strands of love.

Hear angels moan from the constellations above,

tears falling freely while facing the judge.

Homebase (age 16)

Trip over the bag I'm not in the zone,

and ignore the persistent break of my bones.

My decisions are hesitant every step is alone,

and I pause wasting time between third base and
home.

Diving, desperate to catch at least one thing that's
falling,

all I get is a face full of grass,

I'm crawling…

Wheezing,

gasping for breath and rise to my feet,

soul impaled by a bullet of failure and grief.

Misfortune's my name and strength is my skirt,

always so hesitant to cash in my worth.

All these plans, people saw,

the things I should be,

is this what I want? To fulfill their dreams?

I must since I've followed along my whole life,

with no other plans to keep my head up and fight.

So whatever you dream,

or whatever you heard,

just remember I hesitate

between home and third.

Denial (age 16)

She sobs, "I have a confession!"

"Sometimes my pain gets the best of me,
I CRAVE for some presence!
I'm in denial,
my smiles taste of death!"

"I leave a note to a ghost,
let dark petals dance until our love dies.
Note upon note upon note,
voice curling off the page,"
Sobbing so stinking loud!

"I dream of no tears,
of a sweet handsome spirit,
of a father making promises to my face!"

"I have a fatherless Father's Day…"

"My pain was a meadow,
my spirit a cemetery.
And the best of me,
my golden soul,
…burns with revenge."

It Doesn't Matter Why (age 16)

It doesn't matter why no one here understands.

An illusion of illustrations none of them can comprehend,

have been thrust forward into their sight.

The feelings caged inside the soul of a sweet, sinister story,

of a suffering girl.

They don't understand

The fight, the pain,

the loss,

and when she speaks of it they shy away,

like the light had finally been shone onto the monster of a horror movie,

when all she's searching for is a restful shoulder...

One who's soothing.

But all she can find is the abusing words in her own head.

Her thoughts are confusing and breath she's losing,

as she ran and fought,

and fell.

Closer and closer to the abyss of her memories,

sweeping her away like broken glass out of a screen door.

She's pushed off the ledge of her sanity.

Is it possible that people could do such things, to break a person from the inside?

It doesn't matter how many years it's been.

Pain boils in the blood for a long time.

Corrupting innocent children, bewitching them to be driven by indifferent feelings,

instead of the kindness once blooming from their hearts.

Now she hangs crooked, a burnt piece of art,

a crippled shell of a human who was once singing and now screaming.

But the cage she trapped herself in explodes,

metal twisting and bending melting down into roads.

The rusted pipes unclog and overflow a sink that held in so many tears.

A meteor shattering her prison,

and leaving her with nothing.

Yet from nothing,

anything can grow.

My Hero In a Box (age 16)

The most special thing to me is awfully bittersweet

Kept in a box and on display no need to be discreet

He was my brother and my hero he saved me from my fear

He protected me and grew with me our bond truly sincere

Through my childhood and innocence his love gave me more life

Through his later years and slower days he guided me through strife

The younger years were better with each other everyday

The middle years were harder with school and sports in the way

I cried climbing on the bus in the morning, waving to him goodbye

I hugged him in the afternoon seeing the smile in his eyes

The fur on his back had been brushed and petted his tail would always wag

The fur on his belly would be soaked with my tears when I was bruised and sad

He knew my secrets and my goals he was my living
diary

He was my best and truest friend but wasn't human
which was the irony

With him I didn't need the people, the fancy toys and
shows

With everything he had given me it was impossible to
let go

It might be hard to understand how close my dog and
I could be

It might be hard to understand how long he worked to
save me

All I have now are ashes and if anyone dares to mock

I know I can still turn to him, my hero in a box

Claws (age 17)

My family doesn't know about the monster under the floorboards

They don't know it likes to sing and paint and dance

They wouldn't assume it would do anything other than scare me throughout the night

But my monsters claws shine in the sunlight

It's not hidden away in some dark shadow like a coward

It joins me in the day, certain of its place and purpose

It tags along at school

Stalks me in the shower

Spikes my drinks with foul taste and bitter wants

It sleeps with me

Under me

Under my floor calling to me

One cut deep enough can make it go away

But I'm afraid of how deep I'll sink

I may end up dry drowning under the sun

So I peel back my carpet and remind the monster who I am

It's owner

I lock it away under the floorboards

Until I need its claws in my skin

Until dry drowning is the better option than breathing

Bars (age 18)

The bars inside my head are thin, but boy do they hold me in

I climb and spin and try to break them, but they always win

"Try to break them" /you hypocrite/

I'm the one who locked me up

I slow dance with the keys all day until the night refills my cup

And then I spin as a goddess, adrenaline on the pole

The thrill of being young, the fear of being old

I can let go I can slip out, but something keeps me here

Is it trauma, drama, or angst? Or something pathetic as fear?

My comfort zone is my jail and for that I wilt

I watch the movie of my future, let go of what I've built

So should those bars turn to water and one day I slip through

I'd head to town to start my life- oh look it's a saloon

Drowning (age 19)

Most of the time, I'm sucked under, into the dark without air.

Water spilling down my lungs, drowns the flowers that grow there.

But here I lay supported, on an ocean's mystic spell.

With arms spread like a Ravens, I soar across each swell.

My Pen (age 19)

I almost beat a girl once

In the only fight I've ever been a part of

Not my choice

Their words and fists flew at each other

Over me

I was not their target

But I was their consequence

Because one of them broke my fucking pen

They continued their assault on one another

Nails scratching, hair ripping, teeth biting, words
spewing

Whilst I sat there in horror

Ink dripping off my wrists like blood

They broke my pen

My vessel

My only tether to strength and sanity

They had to pay

I stood on one girl's chest stealing her breath

While the other I commanded like a puppet, using her hair as strings

I could have ended them

There was so much wrath in me

b e g g i n g

To be set lose

p l e a d i n g

To be relieved

My vision going blurry with the want

The craving of violence

But this wrath was not for them

Nor was my pens purpose

So I let them go

And I picked up the shattered pieces like I had done my whole life

And moved on

Dear Poe (age 19)

My dearest artful father figure

I too have a muse of pain

Of fear and wrath and bubbling shadows

My own Raven wings beating the air desperate for flight

She knocks on the walls

And my skull

Wreaking havoc in sunlit gardens

Desperately, I hide her from society, so they don't kill her

But I crave to share her so they too can love her

How did you do this?

Your beautiful scribblings give me keys but no answers

I feel as if I am writing blind

And that thrills me even more

Pisxie (age 19)

I fear what certain future there is to come

Her shy giggles are taken as vain taunts

Like what one says and does is not enough to coax her from the mossy nest she's trapped herself in

Her apologies sound stagnant and insincere

Her reassurances feel empty when they land upon your outstretched hands

And you, the pursuer, becomes tired

Agitated

This game is no longer fun

Since it is ongoing with no winner

Because in truth, no matter how much of you she loves

It's her own self-hatred growing the thorns around her

Which bar her inside the prison she's grown inside her mind

Gentle whispers cannot coax

Restless promises cannot persuade

Her stubbornness is her demise

She breaks and re-breaks her own wings

Then cries she cannot fly.

Changeling (age 19)

Her peculiarities were even peculiar for the most
problematic fey.

A damsel dyed in burgundy,

a fire leaking from within.

Such wilted petal plumage,

this Angel graced with sin.

She dons the fruit they bear in her lilac hair,

yet the sweet seed they grow won't pass bruised lips.

For the soil it grows in is spoilt with fungus and toads,

and the clock between realms sardonically ticks.

She coaxes betting cards from Goblins, distracted by
the twinkle in her eye.

The second sight is strong with she, so she chased the
satisfied.

To challenge them and change their will, bend their
desires and mute their muses.

A human lost in Un-Seelie Court has nothing valuable
to lose.

Pout turned purple by soured salt,

glittering stars replace her eyes.

Paper-thin polished wings,

flop to sleep against her spine.

A sapped and scarce changeling,

who's desperate to fly.

Bury (age 20)

There is a gravestone in my mind where my inner child lays

She doesn't rest, she writhes and rolls through all my nights and days

I didn't know what else to do except hide her in that grave

If she was dead and six feet under she was protected from the pain

But her coffin was poorly made, and the earth is eating through

I can feel the pounding of her fists and know that they are bruised

I can't protect what I can't hide, and she's made it crystal clear

She's done pretending that she's dead and will break through my wall of fear

She'll reveal what can't be handled and we'll end up in a cage

Just like the one with grippy socks and bright lights like on a stage

I'm torn between setting her free, to let the world hear her scream

Or keeping her buried and moving on pretending it was a bad dream

Healing her comes at a cost one I don't have the money to pay

So in that coffin she will rot unless the dead will raise

And if that happens I'll pour a drink and salute my wasted effort

Then chug liquid and accept I failed in my endeavor

Shelter Dog (age 20)

My systems in dire need of a cleanse

but I can't ask for what I want if I'm down begging on
my knees

for any kind of company

for a shelter dog like me

we take what we can get, and we are loyal till the end

and in the end we always bend and take the blame

but then we go and do it all again.

Insomniac (age 20)

Do you know why I stay up half the night

why I stop every time I start to write

the reason I run when I turn out the light

or jump to conclusions when you're out of sight?

Do you know what makes me prepare to fight

how my ribs press my heart way too tight

why I listen to wrong reasons instead of right

because I'm busy thinking of the past tonight?

Do you know how my head hurts and feels air-tight

how hard I resist the urge to bite

back the feelings of pain just to be polite

because no one will ask if I'm alright?

Do you know who put out my light

the one who triggers me like dynamite

I feel I've lost my appetite

for my pity party of one tonight?

Do you know when I prayed until midnight

for some god to relieve me of this birthright

to inherit the dark and lose delights

become my pains talented playwright?

Do you know where I float as a satellite

to get away from being treated like a parasite

do you have anything to say after hearing these words
I recite

you think you know me?

No, not even slight.

9am (age 21)

I was drunk by nine am, sitting on the floor of my kitchen thinking

Here I am, on the dirty floor with the cobwebs dreaming

'Bout the future again, what decisions I'll make and regret the next day?

I was drunk by nine am

Where were you at nine am?

Beg (age 20)

Light me on fire

Tear me at my seams

Light pours from my wounds

And my darkness can breathe

Love (age 21)

While in agony he brought forth joy

And while in terror he provided a sense of peace

And despite every effort to not pull him into the tempest of my life

He stepped in with a gentle smile anyway

"Through all your pain

All your anger

And all your fear

I will love you."

The Hidden Garden (age 21)

Can I show you where I've coward?

Where golden petals fought for life,

while water droplets drowned my roots,

and my thorns dripped blood?

Can I show you the garden in my mind?

Can you promise not to steal it?

To not take and take and take,

uprooting me until I'm empty?

Can I lead you to the stone wall,

which limits who can trespass

and limits my escape?

It's high and black and always cold,

and stands in a forest on fire.

The constant autumn outside my walls is nothing
compared to inside.

Even with all her fiery plumage, my autumn is no
match for my gardens spring.

Dark twilights and falling leaves give way to bubbling brooks and wildflower fields.

It's an explosion of art one would not expect from a place as dark as my mind.

Midnight blue and moonshine Morning Glories scale the wall more limber than a human can.

Sunflowers stand guard, while yards of pink Pansies line the footpaths.

The Queen Annes Lace awaits your arrival,

while a crowd of Dragon Lillies and Foxgloves dance,

and Bluebells and Cornflowers sway to a rhythmic beat.

A heartbeat.

Once your toes touch the moss, and you settle yourself down in my soul,

all the bursts of color and light make it hard to find my only hiding place,

at the far side of the garden.

Beyond boxing Cockscomb and Dahlia,

past the Cherry Blossom petals which fall like snow,

and into the woods where gems spill from the earth,

you can hear my heartbeat.

You must navigate the swaying branches of the
Weeping Willows,

duck beneath the wriggling Dogwood boughs,

and find my second wall.

Cracked and grey and grim,

with rivulets of water cascading down the smooth slate
and stone.

In the space beyond is the Rose Garden, growing wild
and untamed.

Bloody petals encourage their thorns to stand proud,

before a tangled mass of Ivy, which chokes the ground
and shields my hiding place.

My leaves are wilted but my petals glow,

a golden rose starved of light,

and lately,

imagining what you would do here, scares me.

Would you rip?

Would you shred?

Or would you slowly poke until your hand found a way through?

If you cannot see me but know I'm there, would you leave me?

Or would you gently massage my roots and break me out of this prison inside my mind?

I'm not grown deep.

I won't struggle for grip.

I want to leave this place and be replanted in the sun where I originally started.

Before the pain.

Before the heartache.

Before adding these stone walls around me was a necessity.

So, can I show you where I've coward?

Can I show you what I've made?

Do you crave the Spring or Fall?

Will you go or will you stay?

We Witches (age 21)

The Crone cackles,

"Oh, my precious gem of darkness.

You are not made for lace, or other pretty little things.

You belong to the glade, to the nightshade, and to the thorns.

Rather than silky ball gowns, you are meant to don the rough pull of corsets,

and feel the sure sway of a blade at your hip.

You are not meant to be the porcelain doll at a dinner party.

You are meant to be the starfire that illuminates in your eyes and burns through your bones.

A gasp of life rather than a breath of pleasure.

Crave to feel your power rather than satisfying your desires.

Stop fantasizing of golden castles and crystal goblets,

of knights in shiny silver foil to pull you from the smoke gulping at your feet.

For we Witches,

we don't play princess."

The Hole (age 21)

My car window broke today

and it made me think of you,

because it's the same exact window

that doesn't work in your car either.

I'll be honest.

These past few months I've imagined

you doing ridiculous and daring things.

Not because I wanted to be swept off my feet.

A tiny bit…

But I want proof you actually care.

Or cared…

But mainly because I just want to be angry.

If I'm angry I don't feel it,

the hole that you left.

But you're not around, so there's nothing for me to be
angry at.

There's just an emptiness where you were

that I'm forced to feel.

Holiday Slumber (age 21)

It was one of those mornings where the gray was slowly washed away by pink.

The birds took their time to rise, following the slow pace of their sky.

Humans did not hum and the earth held her breath.

As autumn gave way to winters death.

Her fires had long been lost to the crippling frost undertone.

And as the sun shyly peeked through the mist of the night, life finally returned to the crow.

Blossoming clouds lit the world from above with the caress of the Yule time snow.

Fugitive (age 21)

Run, run, get out of sight
Flee your home overnight
Cardboard boxes packed too tight
Emotional triggers like dynamite
Children cry while parents fight
Dogs howl before they bite
Strange house with attic frights
Just my first time forced off-site

Once I settled and relaxed
Then again came that ax
Cutting me off my chosen path
At my heels with screams of wrath
Flee the dorm flee the state
Then lockdown and debate
This world round as it collapsed
Losing time as it elapsed

Still again I'm on the run
This game it is becoming fun
Pack my clothes leave the keys
That diamond ring was mine to seize
Once again I've been kicked out
Stuck with baggage, soul, and doubt
Foundations all but have collapsed
For fugitives who beg for scraps

Stockholm Syndrome (age 22)

My cravings are wrong.

Relaxed on damp earth under torn knees, cold wind
kissing my inner thighs, being thrilled while the
darkness closes in on me-

That's wrong.

Drinking tears like mulled wine, or bleach, at ninety on
the freeway begging for the crash to take me-

That's wrong.

The adrenaline rush from the fear, my wrists gripped
so tight circulation pauses, moaning once I feel the
new blooming bruise-

That's. Wrong.

Legs pumping in the woods, not fast enough; wanting
the chase, NEEDING the fight to get off-

That's. Wrong!

Begging to choke rather than for air,

Becoming aroused during screaming matches,

Secretly wishing some bitch would come along and put me in my place-

That's wrong!

That's wrong!

THAT'S WRONG!

I am left unsatisfied when it's safe,

when it's nice.

My body is in ecstasy,

but my mind is in hell.

When I feel sweet release,

I want to cry because I am left void of pain.

And that is wrong.

Allow Your Scars to Bleed (age 22)

After all these years

I must finally allow these scars to bleed

After all these nights

I must finally allow these wounds to breath

After all this compression

I must finally unveil my broken veins.

After all this depression

I must finally unveil my swollen brain

After all these secrets

I must finally let these cuts run dry

After all these times

I must finally let things heal in their own time

After all these fears

I must finally set this darkness free

After all these years

I must finally accept this wickedness in me

Puppet (age 22)

I am on puppet strings for you

Powerless against the cords you pull

The applause is mine but it's obvious you

Are the one in control

I am on thin ice for you

Stark naked against the cold

Not knowing how to compete with the

Pain life hands you in loads

I am in the dark for you

Desperate for your touch but scared

It could be a monster reaching out

I don't know how to be aware

I am on puppet strings for you

That time and time again you snip

And leave me as a useless, broken toy

But I remain there on the floor

A fool

On Being Female part 1 (age 22)

We always have to be happy,

But not too happy or we're annoying.

We always have to be cute,

But not too cute or we're a tease.

We always have to be empathetic and kind,

But not be emotional or over dramatic.

We always have to be sexy,

But not too sexy or we're asking for it.

We always have to be strong,

But not too strong or we're controlling.

We always have to be perfect,

But not too perfect or we're fake.

On Being Female part 2 (age 22)

I looked at a gown that made my imagination and I
lick our lips in synch

"Yes" we thought

"We can take this beautiful thing, edge it up, make it
ours,

"We can bring a little danger to it, awaken its inner
dark charms and evil."

And then it suddenly occurred to me…

this delicious piece of fabric that my eyes savored
seeing and my body craved to wear,

this romantically layered champagne and falling leaves,

I described its sexiness as evil.

Now perhaps that's just my overactive gothic
imagination,

or it's my conditioning kicking in.

The realization that as a woman you learn growing up,

if you wear something like that,

you must watch your step.

If you look that good,

you must choose your words carefully.

If you embrace your sexiness, your beauty, your
gracefulness and don't hold back,

bad things can happen to you.

And there's nothing you can do about it because,

"A dress like that is asking for it."

Physical (age 22)

I want someone to kiss behind my ear.

For teeth to graze and mark my neck,

For someone else's breath to invade my space.

I need chills and sweat but most of all skin,

Undeniable and unrestricted access to skin.

Skin and teeth and hands and tongue and skin.

And air.

I've never needed air more in my life.

I don't want to be fucked.

I want to be craved.

Surgery (22)

I'm in agony

Reliving everything that happened inside me

Emotions so raw it feels like it was yesterday

I need some empathy

Or maybe surgery

Anxiety (age 22)

She holds me in my comfort zone

of shackles and a noose.

Terrified of what I'll see outside

when I think of breaking loose.

Chastise me with the lessons

that have beaten my skin blue:

"Little girls don't want to be your friends,

all they do is torture you."

My crooked back reminds me

of the damage their fists can do.

My aching skull a dull reminder

that what happened was the truth.

A game of She said She said,

6 years of the abuse.

If you think bullying isn't a problem

then you're part of the problem too.

Grasp (age 23)

This is my hand

It's been with me my whole life

Grown with me from a baby to a woman

It's pleasured me

It's pained me

It's healed me

This is my hand

The God of my written world's

And the controller of my life

This is my hand

Meeting (age 23)

Fear sits in my chest

Like a wild, caged beast

Anger keeps her locked in there

And she'll never be released

Sadness borrows time

From Joy and Happiness

And Numb is telling lies

While Humor tries her best

I Knew I Was a Woman When (age 23)

I knew I was a woman when I started to bleed above the knee

The scent metallic and silently present drugged the night to me

When seven days of pain became my savior and my dream

For within the time that I was dry it was not safe to be

A laughing beauty in the dark dancing between the trees

Without the knowledge of the wolf on his continuous hunt for thee

His nose engulfed by the scent of his newest mate to be

Drove him mad and on the prowl desperate to loose his seed

For now a game of moonlit tag became a rush to flee

Caught in fishnets designed to strangle a virgin coral sea

A youthful game to steal one's breath despite their grimacing

A fatal game to steal one's breath and leave the wolf
grinning

I knew I was a woman when I hid my purity from the
thieves

I knew I was a woman when I looked over my
shoulder in my dreams

I knew I was a woman when I could not travel with
less than three

I knew I was a woman, when the men began to hunt
me

Wrongness (age 23)

For once I was a darling girl with innocence pure as snow

Everything I learned was wrong, and I bathe in my wrongness daily in my mind

I keep my wrongness sharp even though my teachers have turned to mist

It is my nature to,

my instinct too,

what I imprinted on at birth.

Coffee (age 23)

I cannot cut

They have my body under lockdown

Under a microscope

Studied

With 24-hour observation

They will catch me

So I cannot cut

I cannot drink

My family knows that pattern

It's absorbed into daily life

Ingrained in our DNA

They will recognize me reflecting their own actions

And will scream at me to stop

So I cannot drink

I cannot run

My hiding places are marked out

In what I write and what I read

Hounds will be on my trail by the end of the day

Because people will know where to look

And they will drag me back

So I cannot run

I cannot die

I have planned to try many times

And as soon as I had the blade, or pills, or rope

My mother would flood my head

Her screams

Her loneliness

I have already put her through enough pain

Mine does not matter

So I cannot die

So how do I release this in me and hide it?

How can I get my fix without being caught and
punished?

Coffee counts as breakfast

It calms down my brain and fills my stomach

It's a habit not hurting my body or bank account

And if people ask me if I've eaten

"Yes, I've had breakfast!"

Is a true and appropriate answer

Therapist (age 23)

I'm so terrified of hurting you I can't bring myself to
start
But here I sit weaving bruises into my black and white
art
When I think my mind gets cluttered
So I shall paint us in reverse
My mother dearest please remember
My love aches within each verse

We buried my place of solace the only human that
knew the truth
And while my heart was hurting, my feelings turned to
you
Another emotional breakdown
Again I was alone
Stuck in an airport between honesty and trying to get
home

Rewind to when my heart was shattered and my brain
not far behind
A diamond ring ripped from my finger, and you took
what pain was mine
We fought till you collapsed
So I dared not relapse
I dared not feel what happened to me at all

Skip back again my pain intense and I thought that you
would see
But instead I had to cover up the fact that I was
bleeding
"You didn't let them win"

"You have proved them wrong"
And now my neck hangs heavy with the medals that
I've won

Now I've traveled back a decade to the week I'd finally
been released
From my hospital prison ward, of which you took my
right to speak
Because honesty would "make it worse"
For you, but not for me
I locked my jaw and smiled, that was the beginning

You did none of this on purpose
But the fact is that it happened
I've helped you my entire life while sacrificing my
needs

I know you did the same,

but that is parenting

The Interview (Age 23)

Nerves are high
While adrenaline battles iced coffee
After dressing to impress but not to show off
You've begun to sweat
But there's air conditioning
You'll be fine

The job you're here for
It's well known
For being underpaid and undervalued
However
They get you with the benefits
And it's mostly work from home

You'll never be bored
Every day will call for the completion of a different
string of tasks
All knotted together in senseless direction

You are provided clear, basic guidelines
But there is absolutely no training
However, that gives you the complete freedom to
forge your own methods that will be most
advantageous to you
As long as you get the job done, it doesn't matter how
That's benefit one

Back to those basics I mentioned, they only include:
Owning a cell phone
Having a valid driver's license
Secretarial duties

Providing housekeeping services
Honing decent cooking skills
Knowledge of basic medical care
Crisis management
And of course providing supplementary income from
a part-time job of your choice

The benefit of this effort is home security
So long as you satisfy the above criteria you should be
provided stable living accommodations

Now those are just the basics
Of course there are opportunities for overtime and
bonuses such as:

If you provide behavioral health services
You could receive medical insurance
If you provide physical therapy
You could receive free meal vouchers
If you provide blind faith and trust
You could receive emotional security
If you consent to sexual labors
You could receive free clothing, jewelry, or other high-
quality gifts

If you bear children or consent to parental duties
You should receive job security as well as all the
previously stated benefits while you raise the offspring
Plus, you might not be expected to work that second
job of yours

Who on Earth would we expect to accept a job this
demanding?
This crazy?
With all these lack of guarantees?

Women.

Awake (age 23)

And here I lie awake

Obsessing over mistakes

You told me that I made when I was seven

I think I should have listened

Because I keep repeating them

"I never asked you to/nobody made you." *(23)*

You. Never. Had. To.

I was born the type of person who automatically would have done ANYTHING for you, for anyone I could.

I was the wall between bullies and children that wouldn't have survived

I was the wall between you and dad, driving him out before he hurt us too badly

I was the wall between you and your parents, keeping their scrutiny at arm's length because you never found a way to cope with it.

I was the golden prodigy,

excelling at everything I touched,

because failing in front of a mother who needed someone to triumph so badly was not an option.

I would have done anything I thought would have helped you,

anything to be worthy of your pride, and would have stopped at nothing to end your pain.

And you're right, you didn't ask that of me or make me.

But you fucking let me.

Mourning (age 24)

Lately, I've been mourning the girl I could have been

Feeling the pain of desires I did not know could be satiated

Until I was too old to let them play

Nightly, my maladaptive daydreams drag me towards the music

Feeling the bass in my chest and the hands on my waist

But I can't lean back into that forbidden embrace

Usually, I can quiet it

The war in my head between peace and adventure

The thrill of letting go

And the guilt of wanting to

Retaliate (age 24)

My mother taught me to not retaliate

That success was the best revenge.

My children will be taught to have empathy,

Be patient,

And give second chances

But if you disregard their boundaries and hurt them…

They'll go for the throat.

Restraint (age 24)

I am terrified of becoming a mother

Now don't get me wrong, it's normal for women to experience some fear

The unknowns of pregnancy

The unmeasurable pains of childbirth

And the pressure of being sent home with a baby that relies solely on you to survive

I experience those fears, but they're not the ones which terrify me

With certainty

I know

That the restraint I displayed my entire life when it came to defending myself

Is something I will not be able to display when it comes to defending my children

Attraction (24)

It's funny

That humans are the only species which shames
females for being attracted to males

When literally

The survival of most other species on this planet

Relies on the male attracting the female

And if he can't

He's useless

Hiraeth (24)

But it was all taken away

And I can't help feeling this way

You should know I have some things to say

Please don't chase my demons away

I'll miss them

Compare (24)

Compare Mother Earth to mothers

We take and we do not replenish

We take and we do not thank

So lie as much concrete as you want

Something will always make it crack

Whether it be roots or water

Energy (24)

I don't have much left to give

But darling, you can have the rest of me

Quote (24)

Violence is not the answer

Until diplomacy fails

Explore (24)

I've always been curious about any ruins I come across in the woods

When did they stop being whatever they were?

And why?

The Result (24)

My life is an oil spill on fire

A man-made natural disaster

That must be endured, until I burn myself out

I was a child battling waves of flame

Gasping for air at the surface

While being burned alive

I was a teenager going under

Forcing myself to drown

Choosing the cold darkness rather than the blinding
flames

I am a woman…

Flailing for purchase way too deep

Struggling to rise from these waters on stained black
wings

But I can hear the sirens call now

And it begs to drown the kings

Time (24)

I want to capture the twilight sun in a glass

So that I may have my golden hour any time I ask

My Mother's Secrets (24)

Your secrets will die with you

I often imagined that once they were gone, I'd lay on my grandparents graves

Upheaving the contents of my soul

Trauma dumping everything put on me by you

And myself

The weight that I carry is like a second skin

I bear it well

But sometimes it slips

And I lose a breath or two

It takes some time to recover, to call upon that practiced smile

To continue on as if I did not nearly fall to my knees under it

I imagined what it would feel like

To be relieved of it

To share it with someone else,

Even if temporarily,

so that I could stretch my aching muscles

I imagined how I would say it so that you wouldn't get in trouble

But now, I can't imagine spilling your secrets

With your parents

With the world

The weight of your pain would be replaced by my guilt

So, there will be no whispers of your truth

No poems of your pain

I was a child, yes

It should not have been my job to help carry it

But it has become part of my purpose here

Because you were once a child too

And it shouldn't have happened

Your secrets will die with me

Outsider (24)

I do not fit in

And I stopped trying to a long time ago

Because even on the hard days,

The loneliness is easier to bear than

The constant rejection

Torn (24)

I have dragged myself through the trenches of hell

I am out

I am mostly healed

I made it

But scraps of me got caught on the barbed wire

Tearing me into smaller pieces than I was meant to be

I got my body out

But I left my skin

My hair

My voice…

So many pieces of me were left

I have already saved myself

But those pieces of me won't relent

They refuse to wither and die

I don't know if I can survive if I don't go to get them back

I don't know if I can survive if I do

Pain (24)

My Father hurt me

More than my Mother ever did

And yet, she's the one I write about

Deep down,

I know it hurts her

When I air out our dirty laundry

But at least I care enough to clean it

When it comes to my Father

I have nothing left to say

The Quitter (24)

I cannot be the only one

Who used their talents as an escape

Rather than a pleasure

And _God_ is it haunting me

As I lay in bed

A soft corpse

I'd rather go back to being a shell

I was empty, sure

But I was strong

My curves were built of muscle and sweat

My lungs could hold out for hours

I would never lose…

But now, just entering a gym insights a panic attack

I have grown soft

Weak

…normal?

My family says it's normal

After all, I'm not a competitor anymore

My body doesn't need to be honed to that degree

But it's the only way I've known my body

And now it's suddenly not that way

And now I'm suddenly always so tired

I don't rise before the sun anymore

So I don't train at all

In the world of athletes, I have become lazy

Passionless

Pushing past the pain

Eliminating excuses

Beating the person next to you

I can no longer find reason to meet those expectations

My success relieves nothing, anymore

So I've quit.